EPIC FAILS

THE RACE TO SPACE
COUNTDOWN TO LIFTOFF

EPIC FAILS

THE RACE TO SPACE
COUNTDOWN TO LIFTOFF

ERIK SLADER AND **BEN THOMPSON**

ILLUSTRATIONS BY **TIM FOLEY**

Roaring Brook Press

New York

To the future

Library of Congress Control Number: 2017958947

Hardcover ISBN: 978-1-250-15061-5
Paperback ISBN: 978-1-250-15062-2

Our books may be purchased in bulk for promotional, educational, or
business use. Please contact your local bookseller or the Macmillan
Corporate and Premium Sales Department at (800) 221-7945 ext. 5442 or
by e-mail at MacmillanSpecialMarkets@macmillan.com.

First edition, 2018
Book design by Monique Sterling

Printed in the United States of America by LSC Communications,
Harrisonburg, Virginia
Hardcover: 10 9 8 7 6 5 4 3 2 1
Paperback: 10 9 8 7 6 5 4 3 2 1

"Those who dare to fail miserably can achieve greatly."

—John F. Kennedy

CONTENTS

INTRODUCTION
"Failure Is Not an Option"

In 1970, Flight Director Gene Kranz told his team at NASA's Mission Control that "failure is not an option." They needed to bring a group of stranded astronauts home from lunar orbit. If Mission Control didn't solve the problem—and fast—the astronauts would die.

But failure is always an option, of course, and there probably isn't a worse place for something to go wrong than in the vacuum of outer space. A human can only survive a few seconds out there without a space suit, and in the 1960s and '70s, the only thing that separated brave American astronauts and Soviet cosmonauts from certain death was a thin sheet of metal and a bunch of technology that looked as if it

came from a cheesy sci-fi movie.

As of 2018, eighteen people have died in spaceflight accidents over the course of history. Thirteen more died during training or in practice missions. The dangers are real. The possibility for failure is always there. But heroic astronauts around the world face these dangers head-on, refusing to let the fear of failure stop them from trying to accomplish incredible things.

The intrepid men and women who go on these missions have all the bravery of the adventurers, explorers, and pioneers who first made important discoveries right here on planet Earth. For them, it was never about violence or conquest, but rather about finding new worlds, exploring the depths of space, and furthering scientific understanding. And, hopefully, using that knowledge to make life better for humanity and our planet as a whole.

Many of the first astronauts had no idea if their new technology could actually carry them into space. The first time anyone had crossed the Atlantic Ocean in an airplane was in 1919, and just forty years later people were orbiting the Earth in outer space. That's not a very long time! These pilots (and most of the early astronauts *were* pilots) were using new tech like jet engines and rockets, fearlessly strapping themselves onto a few thousand gallons of jet fuel and blasting off through the stratosphere at thousands of miles per hour.

But getting the first men into outer space required more

than just the astronauts—it was a team effort that required a massive number of people. On the ground, mechanics, scientists, and engineers all worked together, doing incredibly complex mathematics (*by hand*), and building spaceships out of materials that you could only find in a junkyard today.

The story of the space program isn't about failure not being an option; it's about humanity coming together, knowing full well that failure is *always* an option, and then persevering anyway.

CHAPTER 1
It's Just Rocket Science!

1920

"How many things have been denied one day, only to become realities the next!" —Jules Verne, *From the Earth to the Moon*

Have you ever looked up at the moon and wondered how far away it really is? To the naked eye, it sometimes looks as if you could just reach out and grab it, but the moon is actually 232,271 miles away from us! What's even crazier is that between 1969 and 1972, twelve men actually made it to the surface of the moon and back! That said, it wasn't exactly a smooth journey from the Earth to the moon.

As it turns out, the hardest part of space travel is actually getting off Earth. So far, the most efficient way to escape Earth's gravity is to use rocket propulsion, which is easier said than done.

The first rockets were invented when Chinese alchemists accidentally discovered gunpowder while trying to create an elixir of life. In 1232, the Chinese fought the Mongols at the Battle of Kai-Keng and used rockets on the battlefield for the first time in history. The Chinese Army built weapons that looked (and acted) like gigantic bottle rockets and launched them at the attacking Mongol Army. The rockets weren't superaccurate and probably didn't do a ton of damage, but the explosions, smoke, and fire were so terrifying that the Mongols turned back and fled!

And according to legend, during the mid-sixteenth century, a Chinese official named Wan-Hu wanted to visit the moon. Wan took a wicker chair, strapped forty-seven rockets to it, and planned to use a set of kites to steer himself through the air. On his signal, servants quickly lit the fuses on the rockets, each filled with highly explosive gunpowder. A moment

A depiction of Wan-Hu in his rocket chair, on display at the Marshall Space Flight Center in Alabama.

later, a boom louder than thunder sent everyone around diving for cover. When the smoke cleared, there was no sign of Wan-Hu or his trusty chair.

Needless to say, rocket science has come a long way since then.

Early rockets were based on a simple concept: an aerodynamic cylinder with two fuel tanks, each with a reactive substance that once combined and ignited would create a chemical reaction. The resulting explosion would be funneled downward to create enough lift to compensate for the rocket's mass and propel it upward. Simple, right?

Nope. A metric ton of variables has to be accounted for—including but not limited to temperature, size, weight, design, amount of fuel, durability, weather, etc. The slightest miscalculation could result in catastrophic failure (and in the early days, it often did). In fact, the entire process of perfecting rocket technology is a repeated exercise in failure: make a rocket; launch it; if it blows up, figure out what went wrong; repeat. The scientific method itself is built around seeking out flaws and improving on initial concepts until you have something that works.

In 1895, Russian scientist Konstantin Tsiolkovsky became the first to seriously consider the use of rockets as a potential means of traveling into orbit. He came up with the first equation in rocket propulsion. He theorized the use of mixing liquid hydrogen and liquid oxygen as fuel (way before it was ever possible to do so) and even calculated the speed needed for a rocket to break free of Earth's gravity (which, for those wondering, is about 6.9 miles per second, or 25,020 miles per hour!). This is what is known as *escape velocity.*

In 1903 and 1911, Tsiolkovsky published two volumes of *Exploration of Outer Space by Means of Rocket Devices* in which he explained that a multistage rocket would be needed to achieve escape velocity. (A multistage rocket is basically a launch vehicle made up of multiple rockets stacked together that work in sequence—one after the other.) But few people seemed to notice these incredible revelations until decades later.

Meanwhile, an American physics professor from Massachusetts named Robert Goddard was working on some calculations of his own. In 1916, he sent a proposal to the Smithsonian Institution which theorized how a rocket could operate in space without the need for air. The Smithsonian was so pumped by his research that they sent him a $5,000 grant to see his work in action.

On March 16, 1926, Goddard successfully launched the world's first liquid-fueled rocket. The 10-pound rocket flew 41 feet into the air in just 2½ seconds! Goddard continued to improve his rockets in New Mexico, where, in 1930, he launched a rocket 2,000 feet into the air at 500 miles per hour! Throughout his life, Goddard secured 214 patents, many of which became essential to the development of propulsion technology, and he did it all despite constantly being called a crackpot.

Both Robert Goddard and Konstantin Tsiolkovsky continued to work independently of each other for years. They tried to perfect their rockets with no help or interest from either of their respective governments. Then World War II happened, and the landscape of rocket science changed forever.

CHAPTER 2
Failure to Launch

1942

"The rocket performed perfectly, except for landing on the wrong planet." —Wernher von Braun

Around the 1920s, German engineers entered the scene, testing and developing their own rockets. They were intent on becoming the first in space. In 1927, three Germans—Johannes Winkler, Max Valier, and Willy Ley—founded the Spaceflight Society, an organization that would go on to foster many of the brilliant minds who eventually made spaceflight a reality. One

Von Braun with a model of his V-2

of those brilliant minds belonged to Wernher von Braun, the man who would ultimately chart the conquest of space.

One of the most highly regarded rocket scientists to ever walk the earth, Wernher von Braun is the father of modern spaceflight and a man who dedicated his life to the pursuit of his goal. He earned a doctorate in physics for aerospace engineering from the University of Berlin. Inspired by Robert Goddard's work in the United States, von Braun began to develop his own liquid-fueled rockets. When the Nazi Party rose to power in Germany, however, the Spaceflight Society was dissolved and civilians were barred from firing rockets. In order to continue his research, von Braun reluctantly joined the Nazi regime as the world geared up for World War II.

With the Nazi's, von Braun developed the A-4 rocket, his first full-scale prototype. The A-4 was revolutionary. Von Braun's singular motivation was to launch it into orbit, but the Nazis had something else in mind. The A-4 was renamed the V-2 and reclassified as a "Vengeance" missile.

Von Braun's V-2 looked more like a retro spaceship from a classic sci-fi TV show than a modern rocket. The sleek missile had curved fins and a rounded exterior. At nearly 46 feet tall, a wingspan of 11 feet, and weighing 27,600 pounds, the rocket was a sight to behold. The V-2 would become a prototype for the rockets of the Space Age that would soon follow. Nothing like it had even been attempted before, so of course there was a lot of trial and error—possibly more error than trial.

During initial tests, the V-2 endured every possible malfunction. In February 1942, the first test model slipped out of its restraints and fell two meters, smashing its fins. During the proto-type's second launch, the navigation system failed, sending it spiraling into the Baltic Sea before exploding. The third rocket's nose broke off. Other test rockets flew off course, blew up in midair, or just fell over on the launchpad and unceremoniously exploded. In fact, there were so many problems that the Nazi's suspected von Braun of conspiring to sabotage the rocket program.

It wasn't until October 3, 1942, that von Braun had his first successful launch. The V-2 reached supersonic speeds and traveled 52 miles in the air. Adolf Hitler, however, was unimpressed by the expensive project. He dismissed von Braun's momentous achievement as nothing more than an expensive artillery shell.

As the war waged on, the misuse of his rockets began to wear on von Braun. In 1944, he got drunk at a party and went on about how Germany was going to lose the war and all he ever wanted to do was send a rocket into space. The Nazi secret police arrested von Braun as a traitor, but he was later cleared of charges when the authorities realized that no one else understood rockets as well as he did.

Wernher von Braun was forced to continue his work on the V-2 program as Germany's warheads were loaded and weaponized. To von Braun's dismay, beginning on September 8, 1944, a volley of over 3,200 V-2 missiles were armed with explosive warheads and launched at cities and military installations in Great Britain and elsewhere. He wrote, "The rocket performed perfectly, except for landing on the wrong planet."

When the rockets landed in London, the governments of the world recognized for the first time the truly destructive potential of rocket engineering. But still, they ignored the potential for space travel.

As the war came to an end in 1945 and Allied forces closed in, Hitler ordered that all scientific research and development be destroyed. Von Braun and his fellow scientists weren't ready to give up on their dream, and weren't interested in becoming prisoners of war to the Allied forces. They hoped that they'd be able to use their expertise as a bargaining chip. Together they hatched a plan to escape to the Bavarian Alps, where US troops were advancing.

Germany was divided between the United States and its allies, one of which was the Soviet Union—a large communist state based in Russia that encompassed many current European and Asian countries. The United States and the

Soviet Union emerged from WWII as the two most powerful countries in the world, and as soon as the war with Germany ended, new tension began between these superpowers. The Soviets gathered as many V-2 rockets as they could get their hands on, while the United States secretly imported as many German scientists as they could manage, including von Braun.

CHAPTER 3
Dawn of the Atomic Age

1949

"The cold war would become the great engine, the supreme catalyst, that sent rockets and their cargoes far above Earth and worlds away." —William Burrows, *This New Ocean*

On July 16, 1945, at 5:30 AM in Los Alamos, New Mexico, the Atomic Age began in a blazing nuclear fireball, unleashing 18.6 kilotons of radioactive power. A blinding flash of light—brighter than a dozen suns—lit up the sky, and a shock wave of searing heat burst forth, obliterating everything within its radius for miles. A column

A nuclear explosion detonates at a test site.

of debris bloomed into an ominous mushroom cloud of fallout particles.

J. Robert Oppenheimer gasped in awe, "It worked."

Throughout World War II, America's atomic bomb had been developed in a secret operation known as the Manhattan Project. But its classified status didn't stop Soviet Union spies from infiltrating project facilities and stealing enough schematics to build and test its own nuclear weapon in 1949. The Soviets' getting nuclear weapons was a turning point in history. For the first time, the fate of humanity was at the mercy of two diametrically opposed superpowers with doomsday weapons.

After World War II, both the United States—a capitalist democracy—and the Soviet Union—a communist dictatorship—jockeyed to be the most powerful nation in the world. The Cold War (so called because no actual bullets were fired) that followed was an intense political conflict between the two countries, each flexing their guns in a desperate, paranoia-fueled arms race to build bigger and bigger bombs to prove their ideology was the best.

Militaries quickly began stockpiling as many nukes as they could manage. Atomic bombs

were one thing, but nuclear weapons attached to rockets like the V-2 that could travel hundreds of miles through the air—having that kind of technology changed the game. Both the United States and the USSR (another name for the Soviet Union) immediately began pouring all their resources into rocket research in hopes of building bigger, better, and longer-range nuclear missiles.

As the Cold War heated up, Wernher von Braun got back to work, this time for the US government. Although von Braun wanted to achieve the means for space exploration, he once again found himself building weapons. The US research team, led by von Braun, successfully test-fired its first V-2 in White Sands, New Mexico, on June 28, 1946.

Still, von Braun and his team weren't without their fair share of failures, too. Out of 75 tests, 30 failed. One of the most embarrassing incidents occurred on May 29, 1947, at the White Sands test site. A malfunction caused the Hermes II prototype to lose control four seconds after launch. The Hermes rocket flew wildly off course before crash-landing south of the border—in Mexico! The 4½-ton missile created a 50-foot-wide, 24-foot-deep crater on impact. Luckily, no one was hurt, and Mexico was understanding about the mistake.

Meanwhile, Soviet scientists began to develop their own long-range-missile program.

A NEW ARMS RACE:
The Space Race Begins

Chuck Yeager breaks the sound barrier

On October 14, 1947, fearless pilot Chuck Yeager was strapped into an experimental, rocket-powered aircraft: the Bell X-1. The X-1 dropped free of a B-29's bomb bay, and Yeager ignited the rocket engine above the Mojave Desert. With a powerful sonic boom, at 45,000 feet and over 700 miles per hour, Chuck Yeager became the first human to achieve Mach 1—meaning that he was flying faster than the speed of sound!

Yeager with the X-1. He nicknamed all of his aircraft after his wife, Glennis.

GLAMOROUS GLENNIS

Soviet rocket success

While the Americans were making break-throughs in aeronautics, the Soviets began testing some German V-2 rockets of their own. Their first successful launch came on October 30, 1947. They managed to hit a target 185 miles away!

Launch of an American Bumper rocket 8

First man-made object in space!

On February 24, 1949, the US Army launched the Bumper 5 rocket from White Sands, New Mexico. At an altitude of 244 miles, the rocket became the first artificial object in outer space.

Soviet atomic test

Just a few months later—on August 29, 1949—the Soviets detonated their first atomic bomb. For the first time, the Soviet Union was now on the same playing field as the United States. With both sides building bigger and better weapons, it soon began to look as if nuclear war was inevitable. The only thing stopping it was the knowledge that if World War III started, no one would survive it.

The H-bomb

On November 1, 1952, the United States tested the world's first hydrogen bomb—a thermonuclear weapon 1,000 times more devastating than the original atomic bomb. (It didn't take long for the Soviet Union to catch up.)

Lunar prediction

In 1952, a Soviet magazine predicted that the Soviets would land a person on the moon by the end of the century!

Satellite plans

In 1953, Wernher von Braun proposed putting a satellite into space before the Soviets. Von Braun began to develop a series of Jupiter rockets to do just that. Unfortunately, von Braun never got the go-ahead for launch.

The R-7 makes history

The world's first intercontinental ballistic missile—the R-7—was 112 feet long and weighed over 280 metric tons! It was capable of carrying a three-megaton nuclear warhead a distance of 5,500 miles. After two massive (and expensive) failures, the Soviets made history on October 4,

1957, by launching the world's first satellite into orbit: Sputnik!

The space race had officially begun, and America hadn't even left the starting line.

CHAPTER 4
Sputnik

1957

"We were locked in a battle of democracy versus communism, where the winner would dominate the world." —John Glenn

On October 4, 1957, the Soviet Union launched the world's first satellite into orbit: Sputnik 1. Americans stared skyward in uncertainty as Sputnik circled the globe. To some, it was an omen; to others, it was a challenge. The United States was gripped in fear—if the USSR could put a shiny ball of aluminum into space, it could do the same with a spy satellite—or worse.

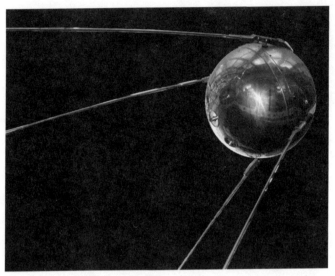

Sputnik 1, the world's first satellite

Sputnik was a small metallic sphere only two feet wide and weighing just 184 pounds. It was launched by a Soviet R-7 rocket into a low Earth orbit, flying at an incomprehensible 18,000 miles per hour and an altitude of 560 miles. It was so fast that it circled the planet once every hour and 35 minutes!

Although the Soviet satellite had barely any function, it was equipped with a small battery-powered transmitter. Not only was it visible from Earth, but Sputnik's radio signal could be heard as it passed by—it let out a faint sound almost like a techno beat, which was pretty scary to people who didn't want a Soviet satellite passing so close to their homes that they could actually *hear* it.

The Soviet press took full advantage of this amazing achievement, stating: "The present generation will witness how the freed and conscious labor of the people of the new socialist society turns even the most daring of man's dreams into reality." Sputnik was, above all else, a propaganda victory.

Then the Soviets added insult to injury when they revealed the sequel, aptly named Sputnik 2. On November 3, 1957, Sputnik 2 launched the world's first animal into space: a dog named Laika. The USSR had left America in the dust.

Throughout the 1950s, three separate branches of the US military had their own rocket programs. The air force had Atlas, the army had Redstone, and the navy had Vanguard, but the public had yet to see any definitive results from these multimillion-dollar programs.

Finally, that December, the United States was ready to launch a satellite of its own.

On December 6, 1957, in Cape Canaveral, Florida, swarms of Americans showed up in anticipation of witnessing America's first satellite launch aboard the TV-3 Vanguard rocket. After two days of delays (from high winds and a frozen valve), the modest rocket was ready for launch. At 11:45 AM, the launch director hit the ignition button.

A gigantic plume of orange flames burst forth. The crowds began to cheer as the rocket started to rise. Two seconds later, the cheers faded as the rocket lost thrust about four feet into the air. The TV-3 rocket—and America's space ambitions—toppled over into a massive cloud of fire and smoke. The *Daily Herald* called it "Flopnik." The *Daily Express* exclaimed "Kaputnik," and the headline of the *News Chronicle* was "Stayputnik."

After this embarrassing debacle, von Braun and his team at JPL (the California Institute of Technology's Jet Propulsion Laboratory) scrambled to answer Sputnik's challenge. Their response: the Explorer 1, a scientific satellite fitted above a four-stage Jupiter C rocket—four-stage meaning four rockets essentially stacked on top of one another to propel the Explorer 1 into space. On January 29, 1958, Explorer 1 was readied at the Cape Canaveral launch site. After some delays, the rocket was finally ready for launch on January 31.

A Vanguard rocket explodes on the launch pad.

At 10:48 PM, the Explorer 1 made history as it lifted off and soon disappeared into the atmosphere. The scientists held their breath as they awaited the satellite's reappearance once it traveled around the globe. Ninety minutes passed, and there was still no sign of the floating hunk of metal. They were ready to call it quits when suddenly something blipped on their radar: Explorer 1 had survived! The satellite had reached a higher altitude than anticipated, so they had underestimated the orbital time of arrival.

Explorer 1 improved on Sputnik 1 in every way. Its scientific instruments were far superior, it did something other than just play techno music, and it managed to stay in orbit until 1970—for twelve years! All the early Soviet satellites crashed to Earth months after their launch.

It was hailed as a victory for the United States, but the applause didn't last long. A few months later, on May 15, 1958, the Soviets launched yet another satellite—cleverly named Sputnik 3—and this one weighed in at 1½ tons. It soon became clear what their next goal would be: putting a man in space.

CHAPTER 5
The Birth of NASA

1958

"It's a very sobering feeling to be up in space and realize that one's safety factor was determined by the lowest bidder on a government contract."

—Alan Shepard

On July 29, 1958, President Dwight D. Eisenhower signed the National Aeronautics and Space Administration (NASA) into existence. Its mission: *"to provide for research into the problems of flight within and outside the Earth's atmosphere, and for other purposes."* NASA was created by an act of Congress, and it was a civilian entity rather than another branch of the military because Eisenhower wanted to ensure that the space agency pursued a scientific endeavor. He also didn't want to make the Soviets nervous that this was a weapons program. The ulterior motive, of course, was to one-up them at their own game.

NASA absorbed the National Advisory Committee for Aeronautics (NACA, the guys behind Chuck Yeager's historic flight), along with resources from Caltech's Jet Propulsion Laboratory, the Langley Research Center, and the army's rocket-research team. NASA's singular goal was to put a man in space. It was the biggest scientific undertaking in America since the Manhattan Project.

Dr. Hugh L. Dryden, the former head of the NACA, made a video announcement to all his employees welcoming them to NASA and introducing them to their newly appointed administrator, T. Keith Glennan (you can watch a video of this on NASA's YouTube page). Over the coming months, it was Glennan who really got the ball rolling, championing elegant simplicity and speed over sophistication. When kicking off the program, all he said was, "Let's get on with it."

Under Glennan's direction, NASA united the nation's brightest minds under one umbrella. Thousands of men and women from all backgrounds were integral to the mission. Decades before cell phones, home computers, or even pocket calculators, NASA employed human "computers"—a workforce of hundreds of female mathematicians who checked and rechecked calculations. One thing that set NASA apart from the Soviet space program when it came to human spaceflight was its commitment to a safety rate of 99.9 percent. The Americans were going to get to space, but they weren't going to lose anybody to do it.

Christopher C. Kraft Jr. became NASA's first flight director. He was given one simple assignment: "Chris, you come up with a basic mission plan. You know, the bottom-line stuff on how we fly a man from a launchpad into space and back again. It would be a good idea if you kept him alive."

No pressure.

Chris Kraft tackled the problem head-on and created the basis for protocols that are still in use today. Before Mission Control was established in Houston, Texas, there was the Mercury Control Center in Cape Canaveral, and it operated on a low budget. It was a makeshift operation in which the most high-tech instruments the flight-control group had were corded telephones, mechanical clocks, and No. 2 pencils. Without the fancy computer readouts of later space missions, the Mercury team relayed information from other sites and kept track of everything manually. Radar and telemetry (flight information) readouts were processed by a massive off-site computer—the size of a building—that was slower than a home PC from the '90s and had less processing power than an iPad.

People often forget that without NASA, we wouldn't have GPS, cell phones, weather forecasts, Facebook, or the ability to watch live broadcasts from the far corners of the globe—all basic modern necessities that we take for granted. During its early years, NASA put the world's first weather satellite into orbit, along with the first television satellite (Telstar) and the first navigation satellite (NAVSAT). Meanwhile, engineers at Langley Air Force Base in Virginia were hard at work designing and testing the latest high-tech spacecraft that would hopefully carry the first Americans into space.

The United States was finally making headway in the space race, but a lot of work still had to be done. Around this time, Edwin Diamond of *Newsweek* magazine wrote, "The first man in space? Most likely a Russian. A mission to Mars? The Russians won't pass up the chance next year. The first man on the moon? He'll be carrying a hammer and sickle."

But what most people didn't realize, however, is that the Soviets also had their fair share of failures; they were just really good at keeping them under wraps. In fact, many of them became declassified only within the past couple of years!

What people were hearing about, however, were the big successes in the Soviet space

Front page of the UK's *Daily Mirror* as the Soviet's success becomes internation news

program. In 1959, the Soviets launched the first "cosmic rocket," Luna 1, which missed the moon's orbit (by 3,700 miles!) and drifted into deep space, but Luna 2 became the first man-made object to crash into the lunar surface. Luna 3 was the first spacecraft to photograph the dark side of the moon, and a few months after that, Venera 1 became the first probe to reach Venus.

The United States was struggling to keep pace, and finally, after months of extensive planning and reorganization at NASA, Project Mercury was a go. Named after the Roman messenger god, Mercury would be America's first foray into human spaceflight. In January 1959, Project Mercury began its thorough search for a team of astronauts with "the right stuff."

Before the Mercury program could take off, however, the Soviets made another historic achievement.

They beat the Americans to space.

On April 12, 1961, Soviet cosmonaut Yuri

Gagarin orbited Earth and made it back in one piece aboard the *Vostok 1* spacecraft. The 108-minute flight had a minor issue on reentry that sent Gagarin spinning out of control, but he managed to eject and land safely. Upon Gagarin's return to Russian soil, the leader of the Soviet Union, Nikita Khrushchev, congratulated him in person. "Let the capitalists try to catch up with our country, which has blazed the trail into space and launched the world's first cosmonaut."

It was another stunning triumph that rocked the world. Moments later, on the other side of the globe, at 5:30 AM, eastern time, NASA's PR chief, Colonel John "Shorty" Powers, woke up to

Vostok 1 sends Soviet cosmonaut Yuri Gagarin up to become the first man in space

a phone call from a reporter. Powers's groggy response was "What is this? We're all asleep down here!" The following day, headlines read: SOVIETS PUT MAN IN SPACE. SPOKESMAN SAYS U.S. ASLEEP.

CHAPTER 6
The Mercury Seven
1962

"It all looked so easy when you did it on paper—where valves never froze, gyros never drifted, and rocket motors did not blow up in your face." —Milton Rosen, Director of Launch Vehicles and Propulsion

It takes a special kind of person to be willingly strapped to an oversize firecracker in hopes of being launched into the vacuum of space. In the case of the Mercury program, seven such individuals were up to the task. The one thing that united them all was bravery and immense calm under extraordinary pressure.

The basic requirements to be an astronaut

were extensive. Candidates needed to be test pilots, under the age of forty, and shorter than five eleven; weigh less than 180 pounds; have an IQ of 130 or higher; and have logged at least 1,500 hours in a jet. Of the 508 men selected for consideration, only 110 actually applied for the program.

After numerous tests, rigorous medical screenings, and a number of stress-inducing psychological examinations, NASA narrowed it down to seven astronauts for its Mercury program. At a press conference in Washington, DC, on April 9, 1959, NASA administrator T. Keith Glennan introduced those fearless pilots to a roar of applause and pride: "Ladies and gentlemen: Today we are introducing to you and to the world these seven men who have been selected to begin training for orbital space flight." A photo of Deke Slayton, Scott Carpenter, Wally Schirra, Gordon Cooper, Gus Grissom, Alan Shepard, and

The Mercury 7 astronauts chosen to be the first Americans in space

John Glenn appeared on the front page of the *New York Times* the next day.

Between training sessions for the mission ahead, the Mercury astronauts witnessed multiple test launches of the rockets that would carry them into space. Unfortunately, these weren't always a success.

December 12, 1959—Titan 1 detonated on the launchpad.

July 29, 1960—An Atlas test rocket disappeared into storm clouds, where it blew up because of structural failure.

November 21, 1960—The MR-1 launch lasted only two seconds before the engines shut down. After lifting off about four inches, the rocket dropped back down to the pad. The rocket stayed put while the top spire of the nose (the emergency escape rocket) blew off and the parachutes deployed out the top.

* * *

At one point, three out of five launches ended in failure. After witnessing one of the Atlas rockets detonate in front of them, Alan Shepard was undeterred. "I hope they fix that problem before they launch us."

He would get the chance to find out soon enough.

After a three-day delay, on May 5, 1961, at 5:15 AM, Alan Shepard climbed aboard the *Freedom 7* space capsule, which was atop a Mercury-Redstone rocket. He wore a shiny 32-pound silver space suit as he was sealed inside the cramped and pressurized metal capsule. The space capsule was streamlined, with a focus on being lightweight enough for the rockets to handle. The cone-shaped capsule was only six feet tall and six feet wide at its base, and it was not a particularly comfortable ride. The Mercury-Redstone 3 was 83 feet high and weighed over 66,000 pounds. The large ballistic missile was a liquid-fueled rocket that was modified to fit the Mercury spacecraft above it.

Alan Shepard was a naval aviator and World War II veteran. He was tough as nails, extremely smart, and really fun at parties. Three weeks before Shepard was scheduled to launch, he got the news that Yuri Gagarin had beat him into space. Immediately, he slammed his fist onto a table so hard that witnesses were worried he might have broken it.

Finally, the time had come to launch—but (as with everything else so far in the space program) not before even more

delays. Alan Shepard sat impatiently in the claustrophobic contraption, waiting for the countdown to rocket him into outer space atop a 30-ton missile. The original launch time had been scheduled for 7:20 AM, but there was a delay because of cloud cover. Once the countdown restarted, it was halted yet again because of a computer malfunction.

After being strapped in for nearly three hours, Shepard realized he needed to use the bathroom. This was problematic, to say the least. The engineers and technicians at NASA hadn't really considered the possibility because Shepard's flight was supposed to last only 20 minutes. Shepard told them he couldn't hold it much longer!

The scientists at Mercury Control argued over what to do. For a brief moment, they considered scrapping the launch, unbolting the door, and dragging him out. Shepard threatened to pee in his suit. Finally, the crew said they could shut down the power so that he wouldn't short out the electrical equipment. At their signal, Alan relieved himself . . . in his space suit. The urine trickled throughout his suit and pooled at his back. After a few embarrassing moments, the countdown started up again.

Then, with two minutes to go, there was yet another delay. Shepard was pretty annoyed. He didn't want to wait any longer. "Why don't you fix your little problem and light this candle?"

At 9:34 AM, *Freedom 7* lifted off the launchpad and soared above the cheering crowds with a bright, powerful explosion that could be felt miles away. Forty-five million viewers watched the live, televised event from home as Alan Shepard left the planet behind. As the rocket climbed into the atmosphere, Shepard felt seven g's of force! (This means seven times the gravity of Earth.) With little control over his flight and only his instruments for visibility, Shepard was at the mercy of the engineers who had designed the hurtling hunk of metal. He was spam in a can. Strapped to a missile.

After 2 minutes and 22 seconds, traveling at an insane velocity of 5,200 miles per hour, the booster engines cut off as planned, and the rocket-assembly separation commenced. For a brief moment, Shepard felt the weightlessness of space. *Freedom 7* had left the atmosphere!

During reentry, Shepard felt g-forces eleven times his own weight, which is more than enough to make many humans pass out. At a ludicrous speed of 15,000 miles per hour and an altitude of about 25 miles, the craft's heat shield absorbed as much as 3,000 degrees Fahrenheit as it reentered the Earth's atmosphere. After a few intense minutes, the spacecraft finally deployed a 63-foot-wide parachute to slow its descent and an air bag to cushion its landing as it headed for the Atlantic Ocean. It was only a 15-minute suborbital flight, but upon splashing down in the Bahamas, Alan Shepard had become the first American in space.

On July 21, 1961, Virgil "Gus" Grissom launched aboard *Liberty Bell 7* for a second suborbital flight.

This time, everything went smoothly until splashdown. For some unknown reason, the capsule's

hatch blew open unex-
pectedly when it hit the
ocean, causing the craft
to fill with water. Grissom nearly
drowned as *Liberty Bell 7* took on
water and sank into the depths of the
Atlantic Ocean. Grissom struggled to stay afloat
in his clunky space suit, but he managed to keep
his head above water just long enough for the
helicopter crew to fish him out.

On February 20, 1962, John Glenn fearlessly
climbed aboard the *Friendship 7* capsule atop
a powerful Atlas rocket. The mission this time
wasn't just to send a man to space—Glenn was
to become the first American to orbit the entire
planet Earth in a spacecraft. A hundred thousand spectators showed up along Florida's
beaches in support of Glenn's historic flight.
Glenn was the Captain America of the Mercury
astronauts, a straitlaced, all-American hero. He

John Glenn posing in front of the *Friendship 7* in 1962. Glenn would return to space in 1988 at the age of 77. Today he is still the oldest person to ever fly in space.

was a Marine fighter pilot during both World War II and the Korean War. He had flown in 149 combat missions. Besides being a decorated veteran, Glenn was also an engineer, test pilot, and instructor. One of his fellow Mercury astronauts,

Scott Carpenter, gave the famous send-off, "God-speed, John Glenn."

10, 9, 8 . . .

The final countdown sequence commenced.

. . . 7, 6, 5, 4 . . .

The Mercury-Atlas 6 rumbled, shedding its icy condensation.

. . . 3, 2, 1.

Liquid fire spewed forth from the rocket's exhaust as *Friendship 7* was hoisted into the sky!

Mercury Control—along with 100 million Americans at home and even the president of the United States—watched the black-and-white footage as John Glenn soared into orbit. As Glenn passed over Australia, he excitedly

John Glenn lifting off aboard *Friendship 7*

reported, "That sure was a short day. That was about the shortest day I've ever run into." The plan was for *Friendship 7* to make seven orbits around the Earth, but something went wrong.

Chris Kraft was at the helm of Mercury Control when a warning light started blinking on one of the control consoles. The light indicated a problem with the landing system. There was a chance Glenn's craft was going to burn up during reentry.

Aboard *Friendship 7*, Glenn noticed the autopilot thrusters caused the craft to drift sideways, so he switched over to manual control to realign it. Mercury Control asked Glenn to check his systems but didn't tell him about the landing problem.

The crew on the ground tried to remain calm as they debated how to proceed. Then they noticed that Glenn's backup oxygen tank had unexpectedly dropped 12 percent and that his fuel supply was also starting to run low. After some back and forth, they agreed it was best to cut the flight short on the third orbit.

When Glenn was informed they were cutting

the flight short, he knew something was wrong. They told him to override one of the systems for reentry. Alan Shepard came on the line and told him there was a chance the landing bag had malfunctioned. John Glenn responded calmly, "Roger, understand."

During reentry, *Friendship 7* became a white-hot ball of fire. As the capsule became engulfed in flame, there was a radio blackout for several minutes. Everyone waited to hear if Glenn had survived. Then the capsule emerged unscathed, and the landing sequence was performed perfectly. The nation hailed his safe return. Glenn had been in orbit for 4 hours, 55 minutes, and 23 seconds. NASA later figured out that the warning light was from a false sensor reading.

Glenn returned safely, but the Cold War was heating up dramatically. With tensions at an all-time high between the United States and the

Soviet Union, President John F. Kennedy gave a
historic speech at Rice University in Texas. The
American people were looking for hope. He gave
it to them.

"There is no strife, no prejudice, no national conflict in outer space as yet. Its hazards are hostile to us all. Its conquest deserves the best of all mankind, and its opportunity for peaceful cooperation may never come again. But why, some say, the moon? Why choose this as our goal? And they may well ask, why climb the highest mountain? Why, thirty-five years ago, fly the Atlantic? Why does Rice play Texas?

We choose to go to the moon! We choose to go to the moon in this decade and do the other things, not because they are easy, but because they are hard; because that goal will serve to organize and measure the best of our energies and skills, because that challenge is one that we are willing to accept, one we are unwilling to postpone, and one we intend to win."

CHAPTER 7

Project Gemini
1965

"The dream of yesterday is the hope of today and the reality of tomorrow." —Robert Goddard

The United States and the Soviet Union had each put men into space—and, just as important, brought them back to Earth alive. But the moon was still 232,271 miles away, and no amount of pump-up speeches was going to get humanity any closer to its destination. That was going to take a lot of hard work, math, science, and experimentation.

In 1961, NASA recruited a second group of astronauts and went to work on a new spaceflight program: Project Gemini. The goal of this mission was to practice and learn as much about space travel as possible but to do it while still orbiting Earth. If something went wrong, it would be a whole lot easier to get home from Earth's orbit than if the malfunction happened all the way out at the moon. Project Gemini was designed to learn about three major challenges that would face a possible moon landing. The first was whether a person in a space suit would be able to go outside his ship, maneuver around, and perform basic tasks, such as repairing the capsule in an emergency. The second question involved whether staying out in space for extended periods would negatively affect the human body.

A moon mission was going to take a couple of days, and if zero gravity did weird stuff to a person's physiology, that might be good to know. The third involved trying to dock two space vessels together while they were both in orbit, which, if possible, would open up a lot of options for planning future moon missions (during the Apollo missions, this technique would be used to reconnect the lunar module with the command module).

The Mercury capsule wasn't great at maneuvering in space, so Project Gemini required a new spaceship. They created the *Gemini* capsule. *Gemini* was larger, designed for two crew members, but a bigger capsule didn't mean these guys weren't pretty squished in there. The ship itself was so small that neither crew member could even stand up during their mission, which doesn't sound like a whole lot of fun when you're stuck in one of these things for a couple of days.

The early missions were designed mostly to test the new ship. *Gemini 1* and *Gemini 2* were unmanned missions, and *Gemini 3* took John Young and Gus Grissom up into Earth's orbit. Gus Grissom named *Gemini 3* the *Molly Brown*, from the Broadway play and movie *The Unsinkable Molly Brown*, referencing the fate of his previous space capsule, which wound up at the bottom of the Atlantic. Unlike Grissom's *Liberty Bell 7*, the most notable thing to happen aboard *Gemini 3* came to be known as the infamous "corned beef sandwich incident."

One hour, 52 minutes, and 26 seconds into the mission, John Young pulled out a piece of "illegal contraband" that he'd smuggled aboard: a corned beef sandwich! "Where did that come from?" Grissom asked.

Young replied, "I brought it with me. Let's see how it tastes." They both took a bite. "Smells, doesn't it?"

"Yes," Grissom said with a mouthful. "It's breaking up. I'm going to stick it in my pocket." They quickly stuffed the crumbling sandwich away before the debris shorted out the space capsule's sensitive equipment.

Disappointed, Young said, "It was a thought, anyway."

"Yep," Gus agreed.

"Not a very good one," Young admitted.

Believe it or not, the corned beef sandwich incident launched a full congressional investigation! The associate administrator for manned spaceflight, George Mueller, assured Congress, "We have taken steps ... to prevent recurrence of corned beef sandwiches in future flights."

Clearly a historic moment for space travel.

Corned beef sandwiches aside, the Americans were making considerable headway toward their goal of being the first to the moon. But the Soviets weren't sitting back and chilling, either. Things really heated up in March 1965, when Soviet cosmonaut Alexei Leonov performed the world's first space walk as part of the *Voskhod 2* mission. Attaching himself to his capsule by a tether cord, Leonov opened the door of his ship, stepped out, and floated freely with nothing but his space suit to protect him from the freezing cold, airless vacuum of space.

News of Leonov's space walk, also known as an EVA (extravehicular activity), came as a shock to NASA. It also came at an incredibly dangerous time, when tensions between the United States and the Soviet Union were coming close to a nuclear war. In 1965, the Americans and the Soviets were providing military and financial aid to opposing sides in the Vietnam War, with the United States supporting the democratic South Vietnamese and the Soviets backing the communist North Vietnamese. Both the United States and the USSR were fighting for any supremacy they could achieve.

So when *Gemini 4* blasted off from Cape Canaveral on June 3, 1965, just three months after Leonov's space walk, the stakes were about as high as they could get.

The Gemini capsules were propelled into space by the Titan II rocket, which is basically a gigantic missile that stood about ten stories tall. The Titan II formed the core of the US long-range nuclear-missile program, but for Gemini the engineers simply reconfigured a few things, removed the nuclear warhead, attached a Gemini capsule onto it, and then used it to blast astronauts Ed White and James McDivitt into space at a couple of thousand miles per hour.

NASA monitored the mission from its brand-new Manned Spacecraft Center in Houston, Texas, as White and McDivitt began their preparations for the EVA. As *Gemini 4* orbited more than 100 miles above Hawaii, McDivitt kept an eye on the flight controls while Ed White

Astronaut Ed White taking the world's first "space selfie"

pulled the hatch open and ejected himself from the spacecraft with only a 25-foot-long tether hooking him to the ship. Everyone held their breath as White, an air force pilot who had

Ed White during his EVA

logged over 2,000 hours piloting jet aircraft, slowly drifted toward the blackness of space. Then the radio transmission came in. White said, "I feel like a million dollars!"

Zero gravity isn't easy to move around in, so White tried to navigate using a remote control attached to an oxygen tank he had strapped to his chest. When he pulled a lever, O_2 would shoot out of the tank (kind of like a jetpack) to move him around. Unfortunately, the tank wasn't really all that big; it held only about three minutes of propulsion.

Because Ed wasn't ready to come back, he just pulled on the tether to maneuver himself around the ship and keep hanging out in space. You'd have to be pretty brave to pull yourself around on the one thing that is standing between you and certain death, but you also have to be pretty brave to be an astronaut in the first place, so this makes sense.

After a 20-minute space walk, White finally came back to *Gemini 4*. But there was a problem—the hatch wouldn't close!

Wearing big astronaut gloves, operating in almost complete darkness, Ed White and James McDivitt suddenly realized both of their lives were on the line. They pulled, fought, and struggled to get the hatch resealed. With that thing open, both men would burn to death on reentry to Earth's atmosphere.

We have to imagine that the *hiss* of that hatch finally locking shut was one of the greatest and most relieving sounds those guys ever heard in their entire lives. Finally, they completed their mission and returned home in one piece.

The first American space walk had been a success. But that faulty hatch wouldn't be the only problem the Gemini program would run into.

The next one was a doozy.

CHAPTER 8
A Dangerous Rendezvous
1966

"We have serious problems here. We're tumbling end over end. We're disengaged from the Agena."

—Astronaut David R. Scott, *Gemini 8*

On March 16, 1966, more than 100 miles above the Earth, command pilot Neil Armstrong carefully guided the *Gemini 8* capsule toward the Agena Target Vehicle. With both ships orbiting the planet at over 18,000 miles per hour, Armstrong adjusted his thrusters and made his final approach. It was Neil Armstrong's first flight into space, and it was the first time in

Neil Armstrong, before the *Gemini 8* mission

history that a spaceship ever attempted to dock with another.

Nobody was inside the Agena. It was an unmanned craft. Think of it as a modern-day drone except built using roughly the same amount of technology you would find in a modern handheld calculator. The Agena had been launched before *Gemini 8* and had spent its time orbiting Earth collecting space dust that could be analyzed later. Now, in humanity's first test of ship-to-ship docking, astronauts Neil Armstrong and David Scott were going to try to hook up to it.

Armstrong would dock the ship, then Scott would climb out of the *Gemini* capsule, EVA over to the Agena, collect the space-dust samples, and bring them back to *Gemini 8*.

Of course, docking with a spaceship isn't as easy as snapping a couple of LEGOs together. Both ships were flying in orbit high above the Earth, traveling at incredible speeds, and there was zero room for error. But Neil Armstrong wasn't an ordinary pilot. This guy had earned his pilot's license at the age of sixteen, flew seventy-eight combat missions in Korea, and logged over 3,000 hours flying over 200 different aircraft, including quite a few experimental fighter jets, like the X-15, a hypersonic rocket-powered aircraft that traveled six times the speed of sound!

According to his kids, it was tough to watch movies with Armstrong because every time they showed the inside of an airplane, he would say something like, "that's not what the inside of that kind of plane looks like." And Neil Armstrong would know—he'd flown basically every dang plane on Earth and could remember what their control panels looked like.

Using incredible skill, Armstrong slowly guided *Gemini 8* toward the Agena, making slight changes on his maneuvering thrusters to ensure everything lined up just right. Then, with amazing precision, Armstrong hooked *Gemini 8* to the Agena, linking two spacecraft together for the first time in history.

However, the second they connected, a loud noise ripped through *Gemini 8*, and with a terrifying jolt, the entire world started spinning for both astronauts. In moments, *Gemini 8* was tumbling completely out of control!

The view outside became a blur of motion as *Gemini 8*, still attached to the Agena, spun in what is probably the most epic barrel roll ever recorded. Whipping around at one full rotation per second— an unbelievably fast speed—Armstrong and Scott twirled like a fidget spinner. Some-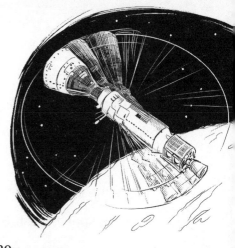thing was very wrong, but neither man knew what it was or how to stop it.

But if there's one thing you should know about astronauts, it's that it takes a lot to freak them out. The world was spinning around them, and the g-force of the spins was causing both men to come very close to blacking out, but Scott and Armstrong still calmly talked on their intercoms to each other and to Mission Control. They disengaged from the Agena, but the spinning continued.

Thinking quickly, the men realized it wasn't the Agena that had malfunctioned; it was actually a failure in one of the thrusters on *Gemini 8*. Apparently, one of the maneuvering thrusters had activated and not turned off, and now it was pushing the men into an even faster spin. They shut that thruster off, but because they were in space, just turning off the thruster wasn't enough to stop the spin. If the crew of *Gemini 8* didn't do something soon, both men would pass out and quite possibly never wake up again!

Neil Armstrong did the only thing he could think of. Despite blurry vision and dizziness, Armstrong fired all sixteen reentry thrusters, powering them all in the direction against the spin. The capsule slowly stopped, and the crew were safe—for now.

There was a new problem: Armstrong had burned

75 percent of the fuel for thrusters that *Gemini 8* was going to need to reenter Earth's atmosphere. *Gemini 8* had been in space for only 10 hours of the mission's planned three-day schedule, but now the astronauts needed to turn back for home—immediately—and seriously hope that they had enough fuel left to arrive safely.

There was no time to waste. Armstrong and Scott were flying over China at the moment, nowhere near the Atlantic Ocean, where they were supposed to land, but there was no other option. The air force and navy scrambled their rescue teams to try to get to the landing site, which was now far across the Pacific Ocean. Everyone held their breath as Armstrong guided the capsule toward Earth and began descending through the atmosphere.

Everyone breathed a sigh of relief when *Gemini 8* reported it had splashed down safely. Air force divers parachuted into the water and attached a flotation ring to the capsule, but it still took a few hours for US ships to come and pick up the astronauts.

Thanks to quick thinking and an unbelievable amount of coolness under pressure, the crew of *Gemini 8* had returned home safe and sound.

The docking mission itself was a pretty Epic Fail, but it had been a controlled one. It's one of the reasons the Gemini program existed—to make sure that any failures would happen close to Earth, and not all the way out in deep space. It proved that docking was possible, and that a lunar lander could redock with a spaceship, but more testing, more design, and more research were needed before something like that was going to be attempted farther from Earth.

As for Neil Armstrong and his amazing heroism under duress, just remember his name. It won't be the last time you see it in this book.

CHAPTER 9
Tragedy
1967

Ad astra per aspera. —Latin proverb,
meaning "A rough road leads to the stars"

With actual moon missions now firmly in
NASA's sights, both the United States and the
USSR began pushing themselves to the limit in
hopes of being the first world power to put a
person on the lunar surface. Unfortunately, this
rush to be first caused both countries to get
sloppy, and this led to extreme tragedies on both
sides.

The follow-up program to Gemini was known as Apollo—named after the mythological Greek god of the sun. Because the Apollo missions were designed to be in space for extended periods, land on the moon's surface, and then get the astronauts back home safely, a larger ship would be needed. So Wernher von Braun and his team began work on creating the largest and most powerful rocket the world had ever seen: a behemoth known as the Saturn V.

The *Apollo Saturn V* spacecraft basically was designed to work like this: A command module and service module (called the CSM when combined, or the CM and SM when separated) would be loaded with a three-man crew, attached to a lunar landing module (LM, pronounced "Lem"), and then all that would be stuck on top of a ginormous 363-foot, three-stage Saturn

V rocket and blasted into Earth's orbit at incredible speeds.

Once the first stage of the Saturn V rocket was out of fuel, it would break off, and the CSM/LM would circle the Earth twice, still attached to the second stage of the Saturn V. If all systems seemed to be working okay, the Saturn V would engage stage-two thrusters and blast toward the moon at thousands of miles per hour. When stage two ran out of fuel, it would break off as well, leaving just the CSM/LM hurtling toward the moon.

After two or three days' journey, the CSM would arrive in the moon's orbit. Two of the crew would then get into the LM, land it on the moon (not an easy task), and then walk (bounce) around to see what it was like. Once the astronauts on the surface planted a flag and collected some moon rocks, they'd get back into the LM and blast back into orbit. The astronaut in the

CSM would find the LM in orbit, dock with it (this is why docking was such a big part of the Gemini program), and bring the crew back aboard the CSM; and then the CSM would disconnect the LM and fly back to Earth by itself. The CSM would spend another two or three days hurtling back toward Earth, enter Earth's orbit, and parachute into the ocean to be recovered by the navy.

That was the plan, at least.

If that sounds incredibly complicated, that's because it was. Keep in mind, also, that these guys are doing this twenty years before the invention of the first Mac computer. Rocket scientists were still solving complex physics and calculus equations *using a pencil and paper.*

NASA spent months testing the rocket systems and training the first astronauts to undertake an Apollo mission. The crew it settled on were Gus Grissom (the second American in space), Ed White (the astronaut who did America's first space walk), and Roger B. Chaffee, a pilot who had been in Mission Control for a number of Gemini missions. *Apollo 1* was scheduled to launch on February 21, 1967—the first test run of a mission that hoped to put an American on the moon.

But the mission never launched.

On January 27, 1967, during a systems test in Cape Canaveral, the three astronauts of *Apollo 1* entered the CSM to perform a full systems test. During the test, an electrical power failure created a spark that ignited the oxygen-rich environment of the CSM, immediately becoming a raging fire that spewed thick black smoke throughout the cockpit. The crew, still strapped into their seats, were unable to eject through the hatches before they succumbed to the smoke and fire. The emergency hatch wouldn't open because it had been designed not to blow open accidentally as it had during the *Liberty Bell 7* mission. All three men died. They would be the first Americans to die in the space program, and the loss of these heroes completely shocked and saddened the entire country.

Three months later, the USSR had a tragedy in its lunar program as well. The Soviet leadership knew it had fallen behind in the space race, so instead of pursuing its own version of Project Gemini, it went straight into an attempt to build a lunar landing module. The Soviet moon-landing program was based around the *Soyuz* spacecraft. It had a two-man crew, complete with a landing module that would send one member of that crew to the surface of the moon. In their rush to make such a gigantic leap forward in their program, however, the Soviets ended up pushing

The crew of *Apollo 1*

themselves beyond what many of their cosmonauts believed was safe.

On April 23, 1967, *Soyuz 1* launched. Its pilot was veteran cosmonaut and hero of the Soviet Union Vladimir Komarov, a man who had commanded the historic *Voskhod 1* mission three years earlier. *Soyuz 1* ran into trouble almost immediately. As soon as the ship reached Earth's orbit, it was supposed to deploy solar panels to collect energy from the sun, but one of the panels failed to open because of a mechanical error.

Komarov stayed cool under pressure, but then a thruster malfunctioned as well, causing *Soyuz 1* to start spinning as *Gemini 8* had. Komarov used a strategy similar to Neil Armstrong's to quickly correct the roll, but as you can probably imagine, he wasn't really too excited about hanging out in space in a craft that had already malfunctioned twice. He aborted the mission and reentered Earth's atmosphere.

Unfortunately, his ship let him down a third time. Its parachute didn't open.

Komarov fired *Soyuz 1*'s backup chute to try to slow the craft's speed as it careened toward Earth, but the reserve chute got tangled up and didn't deploy correctly. *Soyuz 1* crashed into the Russian countryside and exploded.

Komarov would be the first person to die on a spaceflight mission.

Together, these tragedies almost killed the space programs of both countries.

But the brave astronauts who had performed these dangerous missions over the last six years hadn't come this far just to lie down and quit with the moon so close in their sights. Every astronaut knew this was dangerous, groundbreaking work that no human had ever attempted before, and they knew they were putting their lives on the line every single time they heard the phrase *blast off*.

If flying to the moon was as easy as sitting on your couch playing a sci-fi spaceship video game, anyone would be able to do it.

These astronauts and cosmonauts weren't just anyone. They were pioneers. They wanted to break barriers that had existed for millennia, explore new lands, and do the things that no-body had ever even dreamed was possible. And that's not always safe.

Instead of giving up, both nations took the next year and a half to improve, redesign, and reorganize their missions. The United States launched *Apollo 2* through *Apollo 6* as unmanned tests of the equipment, and the USSR dedicated all its resources to improving the *Soyuz* craft. Both the United States and the USSR were intent on their desire to reach the moon, but not at the expense of human life. Both countries had suffered horrible catastrophes and would do everything they could to make sure it would never happen again.

CHAPTER 10
Apollo
1968

"Shoot for the moon; you might get there." —Buzz Aldrin

On October 11, 1968, the Saturn V rocket carrying *Apollo 7* tore through the skies above Cape Canaveral. Just a year and a half since the tragedy of *Apollo 1*, the United States was launching its first manned space mission since the disaster.

Apollo 7 was the first time the Apollo program had been into space with a three-person crew. The objective of the mission was to test the *Apollo* spacecraft and see how it held up. This must have been more than a little nerve-racking for the crew inside of the ship. However, astronauts Walter Schirra, Donn Eisele, and Walter Cunningham were both incredibly brave and competent. They moved forward in their mission without any hesitation.

The *Apollo 7* crew separated the stage-two rocket (they weren't going to need it to propel them to the moon) and fired off the engines on the CSM. And, for the most part, everything worked out great! The windows of the CSM fogged up a little bit, and it was difficult to poop in the CSM because you had to take your entire space suit off to do it, but there were a lot of fun parts, too. The crew took a video camera with them and sent videos of their adventure back to Earth. Kids across America could write letters to the astronauts, and then the astronauts would answer their questions live from the spaceship.

Apollo 7 practiced docking and maneuvering, then parachuted safely back to Earth. The capsule landed in the Atlantic and flipped upside down, but when the craft's flotation bags inflated, they flipped it right side up again. (Whew!)

Apollo 7 had proved that the craft worked. Now it was time to go for the ultimate goal.

Commander Frank Borman and astronauts Jim Lovell and Bill Anders lifted off on December 21, 1968, aboard the historic *Apollo 8* mission. Their goal? Become the first humans to travel to the moon.

Apollo 8 reached Earth orbit, powered up its

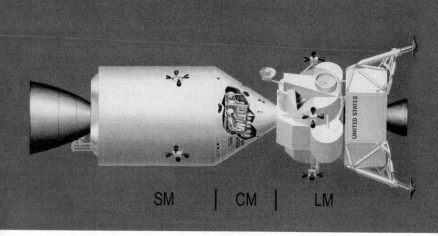

Diagram of the components of an Apollo craft

thrusters, and blasted out into space. After 68 hours, 58 minutes, and 45 seconds of travel (over 2½ days), the *Apollo 8* CSM finally entered lunar orbit. While orbiting the moon, the astronauts became the first people to see the dark side of the moon (no Transformers were there), and they saw the first "Earthrise" as it came into view.

Over the next 20 hours, the crew orbited the moon ten times, taking pictures, drawing maps, and trying to identify good landing sites for future missions. They also sent a couple of video transmissions back to Earth, which were broadcast on every TV in the world. The most famous of these was on Christmas Eve as Earth came into view over the lunar horizon. You can watch all these videos on YouTube!

After visiting the moon, the Earthlings engaged their thrusters and began the long return trip home. They reached Earth and reentered the atmosphere, screaming in at an unbelievable 24,000 miles per hour. The heat from the atmosphere was so intense that the outside of the Apollo capsule reached temperatures of over 5,000 degrees Fahrenheit. They splashed into the Pacific Ocean after 147 hours on their mission and were received as true heroes not only in America, but across the globe, too. Borman would receive a Congressional Space Medal of Honor for his heroism, and all three astronauts were recognized as "Men of the Year" by *Time* magazine.

NASA's work wasn't done yet, however, and

the next two Apollo missions would test the CSM and LM. *Apollo 9* spent ten days in Earth orbit, ejected the LM, tested the LM's thrusters, and then successfully redocked it with the CSM before returning home. *Apollo 10* repeated *Apollo 9*'s testing, but at the moon, where the crew sent back the first color TV footage of the lunar surface. This mission also ejected the LM, but the astronauts inside descended to about nine miles above the lunar surface before returning to the CSM and heading back to Earth.

Amazingly, despite all the hardships, failures, and trials that humanity had faced on its long, difficult quest to reach the moon, the impossible was now in our grasp. Putting a human on the moon was now a real possibility.

The only thing left was to do it.

CHAPTER 11
One Small Step, One Giant Leap

1969

"There can be no great accomplishment without risk."

—Neil Armstrong

It was around 1:45 PM, eastern time, on July 20, 1969. Through the main window of the LM, astronauts Neil Armstrong and Edwin "Buzz" Aldrin peered intently through the darkness of space toward the white rocky surface of Earth's moon. With a sudden jolt, the LM disconnected from *Apollo 11*'s CSM. From the cockpit of the CSM, pilot Michael Collins radioed in that everything looked normal on the LM and gave the okay for Aldrin and Armstrong to begin their descent to the lunar surface. With a steely gaze, Neil Armstrong took the controls of the LM and prepared to make history.

But as with many things so far in the quest for the moon, nothing was going to come easily.

Suddenly, without warning, all the lights and alarms on the LM console came screaming to life. Aldrin and Armstrong checked the gauges

and readouts of their craft, trying to make sense of the flashing beacons and earsplitting Klaxons that were beeping across the board. Quickly and calmly, Neil Armstrong realized the problem: Too much telemetric data were coming into the LM all at once, and the LM didn't have the capacity to process all the calculations and data it was receiving. Remember, this thing might have been 200,000 miles from Earth and about to land on the moon, but it had less computing power than a solar-powered calculator.

The noise was deafening. All his console readouts were scanning line after line of gibberish. And, all the while, the moon loomed larger beneath the landing craft.

But Neil Armstrong hadn't come this far just to turn back now. He wasn't about to let a potentially catastrophic equipment failure stop him from achieving his mission.

So, in the face of all this chaos, he did something completely amazing: He turned off the onboard computer. He was going to bring the spacecraft down manually.

Thirty-eight-year-old Neil Armstrong gripped the controls of the LM, drawing on decades of piloting experience as he carefully guided the LM toward the lunar surface. Sitting atop a few thousand gallons of jet fuel in an aluminum coffin that possessed all the computing power of a microwave oven, Neil Armstrong hurtled toward the lunar surface at over 60 miles per hour. He was trying to land on a celestial body that no human had ever landed on before. For the next 10 minutes, he used his landing thrusters to slow his descent, maneuvering side to side to ensure that the craft landed upright, didn't tip over, and didn't crash in a huge, fiery explosion. One mistake, one false move, and Armstrong and Aldrin would have been stranded on the moon with no way to escape.

It was kind of like the most dangerous video game ever played, even though the first real video game ever invented, *Pong*, wouldn't be released until three years after the *Apollo 11* mission.

At 4:18 PM, eastern time, the *Apollo 11* LM (radio call sign *Eagle*) touched down safely on the surface of the moon in a nice flat place called the Sea of Tranquility, with only 20 seconds of fuel left in the landing thrusters.

Armstrong confidently radioed in to Mission Control his famous line, "Tranquility Base here: The *Eagle* has landed."

Everybody at Mission Control let out a resounding cheer and started clapping and high-fiving one another.

It took a little over six hours for Armstrong and Aldrin to rest, put on their space suits, and get geared up to walk on the moon. To capture the historic moment, the LM deployed a TV camera, which broadcast live to 530 million people all across planet Earth—nearly a sixth of the human population, all watching in astonishment and awe as astronaut Neil Armstrong climbed down the ladder of the LM and triumphantly became the first human ever to set foot on the surface of the moon.

The words he spoke as he stepped off the foot of the ladder are remembered today as one of the most iconic quotations in human history:

"That's one small step for man, one giant leap for mankind."

For the next 2½ hours, Neil Armstrong and Buzz Aldrin walked on the moon. They noticed it had less gravity, which allowed them to travel easily by jumping long distances rather than slogging along like all those chumps back on

Buzz Aldrin during the *Apollo 11* mission

Earth. They set up some scientific equipment to gather data on the moon, collected about 47 pounds of moon rocks, planted a US flag, and took the picture that is probably best known today as the statue given to artists who win

MTV Video Music Awards. They left behind a plaque commemorating world peace and another one listing the names of all the astronauts and cosmonauts who had died during the quest for the moon. They also spoke to President Richard Nixon on the phone and set up a laser rangefinder that provided an exact distance between

Buzz Aldrin poses with the American Flag during *Apollo 11*

the Earth and the moon: 232,271 miles. For a frame of reference, that's the same distance as flying all the way around Earth—almost ten times!!!

After completing their mission on the moon, Aldrin and Armstrong reboarded the LM, blasted back up into lunar orbit, and docked with

Michael Collins in the CSM. The crew all transferred aboard the CSM, jettisoned the LM into space, and then headed back to Earth.

After a grand total of eight full days in space, the crew reentered Earth's atmosphere and parachuted safely into the Pacific Ocean. All three astronauts were quarantined for three weeks, just to make sure they didn't get any weird moon diseases. Once it looked as if everything was okay, they were lavished with parades, medals, and even a star on the Hollywood Walk of Fame. The moon landing had, at the time, been the most watched television program in the history of the world. Collins, Armstrong, and Aldrin met the US president, the pope, and the Queen of England and received medals of honor from seventeen countries. Now there are craters on the moon named after each of these heroic men.

CHAPTER 12

We Have a Problem

"It really was not until I looked out the window and saw the oxygen escaping from the rear end of my spacecraft that I knew that we were in serious trouble." —Jim Lovell

It was just a few minutes after 9 PM, eastern time, on April 13, 1970, and the crew inside the *Apollo 13* CSM were just winding down after broadcasting a tour of their ship live on national television. Astronauts Jack Swigert, Fred Haise, and Jim Lovell had spent the last hour carrying a TV camera around the CSM and LM, showing off in zero gravity, answering questions, and talking about all the cool stuff that was going on during their quest to become the third mission in history to land on the lunar surface. They'd been in space for over two days and were now more than halfway between the Earth and the moon. With the excitement over, the crew settled down to perform a little bit of routine maintenance as they rocketed toward their objective.

From Mission Control in Houston, Jack Lousma radioed in a few "housekeeping" items for the crew to take care of before bed. They were asked to power down a couple of systems, run a diagnostic on a couple more, and then stir the tanks containing the liquid oxygen that *Apollo 13* was using for fuel to keep it from freezing.

And that's when a nice, quiet night in the CSM suddenly became an epic struggle between life and death.

A split second after Jack Swigert flipped the switch to stir the cryo tanks, the entire spacecraft was rocked by a huge explosion. As alarms screamed and the entire control board flashed a crazy variety of colors, astronauts Swigert, Haise, and Lovell all immediately sprang into action, knowing that even the smallest hole in their vessel would mean al- most instant death.

They radioed in to Houston, re- porting that all the gauges were flipping out—a number of crucial  systems were offline, and the ship was starting to rock and jerk around like crazy. The onboard computer had gone to an automatic restart and was booting back up again. Unsure what was happening, *Apollo 13*'s call to Houston is now one of the most famous quotes in the history of spaceflight:

"Houston, we've had a problem."

In the following few minutes, the astronauts calmly but quickly relayed to Mission Control what they were seeing, while the crew on the ground tried to figure out whether this was a computer malfunction or something worse. Astronaut Jim Lovell's immediate thought was that the LM had been hit by a meteor, so he ordered the hatch to be shut between the CSM and the LM, but upon looking out the cockpit window, he saw something much more terrifying:

The *Apollo 13* spacecraft was venting gas into space.

Jim Lovell was no stranger to spaceflight. He had flown *Gemini 7*, been on *Gemini 12* with Buzz Aldrin, and piloted the CSM during the *Apollo 8* mission that orbited the moon for the first time. He was a pro and had iron nerves, but he also knew this was really bad. If the crew of *Apollo 13* were going to get out of this alive, they were going to need to work quickly.

At the time, nobody knew what had happened to the SM, but we now know that one of the wires in the fuel cell oxygen tank had short-circuited and sparked, igniting oxygen in the tank and creating a big explosion. Oxygen tank 2 was destroyed, oxygen tank 1 was leaking gas into space, and fuel cells 1 and 3 had failed.

In short, *Apollo 13* was 200,000 miles from Earth, and it had just lost most of its light, water, and electrical power. With one flip of a switch, the mission had gone from "become the third group of astronauts to set foot on the moon" to "how are we going to get these guys home alive?"

The CSM was dying, leaking fuel and gas, so the first thing to do was to shut it down and move the crew into the LM, which luckily was undamaged by the explosion. Swigert, Haise, and Lovell powered up the LM as quickly as possible, performing a job that usually takes hours in just 15 minutes, and then, before transferring, they shut down all power in the CSM completely—something that had never been done in space before, and something that was seriously not recommended. Whether they'd be able to power the CSM back up again for reentry would remain to be seen. But that was a problem to deal with later.

Back in Houston, NASA teams scrambled to think of ways to get these men home alive. Flight Directors Gene Kranz, Gerald Griffin, and Glynn Lunney mobilized teams to work around the clock to figure out new scenarios for getting *13* back to Earth on limited power. Flight plans for NASA typically took months to put together and required a ton of supercomplicated mathematics, but Mission Control didn't have that kind

Gene Kranz at Mission Control during the *Apollo 13* mission

of time. The LM was designed to support two astronauts for two days; now it was going to have to support three men for four days!

Getting back wouldn't be as easy as just "turning the ship around" and flying back to Earth. Altering course like that would take a ton of fuel and power, and *Apollo 13* didn't have much of either. So instead of turning around, NASA decided to continue to the moon, take one orbit around it, and then use the gravity from the moon to "slingshot" *13* back to Earth. This would take longer, which was bad because the astronauts had limited food and water, but it would use less power and fuel and give *13* the best chance of getting back.

Unfortunately, this change of plans was going to require two major course corrections, and those corrections were going to have to be done from the LM, not the CSM.

Because nobody knew exactly what the damage was to the CSM, it was too risky to fire up the engine. NASA decided to do the correction by firing the LM engine—even though that was designed only to land on the moon, not to propel the spacecraft through outer space! Plus, not only did they not know if this would work, but the LM was at the back end of the craft, and all the navigation equipment was in the CSM. Still, using a computer for visuals, which had never

been done in space before, Fred and Jim worked together to get the craft moving into a path that would take it around the moon. Jim later said that it was "like learning how to fly all over again." No pressure, right?

Miraculously, Jim Lovell and Fred Haise got *13* onto course. Once everything looked good, the crew then had to shut down power to the LM as well. They were going to need that battery power later. For the next couple of days, the entire *Apollo 13* spaceship was running on 12 amps of power. Most regular hair dryers run on 15!

There was plenty of oxygen on board the ship, but the LM was designed for only two people. Three people were producing too much carbon dioxide in the cabin. Carbon dioxide (CO_2) is the stuff that we exhale, and in large quantities it can be deadly. To "scrub" out the CO_2, the crew were going to need the bigger CO_2 scrubbers in the CSM, but there was a problem: The CSM scrubbers were square, and the LM scrubbers were round. To plug a CSM scrubber into an LM socket, they were literally going to need to put a square peg into a round hole.

Luckily, they had an entire team of NASA engineers to help them do just that.

Back in Houston, a team of NASA geniuses figured out a crazy way to jury-rig a bizarre-looking device they called the "mailbox," which would convert the square scrubber to the circular hole. Using cardboard, plastic bags, hoses, and, of course, duct tape (because duct tape fixes everything), the engineers put something together, radioed the astronauts how to build it, and then the crew of *Apollo 13* had to do it in zero gravity. And you know what? They did.

Water was also a problem, since a lot of it had been blasted into space during the explosion. The astronauts were having to live on *six ounces of water a day*—less than one cup. Having the power off made the LM totally freezing; temperatures dropped as low as 38 degrees! Condensation from the cold and the astronauts' breath covered everything, including the equipment panels. Cold, hungry, thirsty, and exhausted, the astronauts were so miserable they couldn't even sleep when they were tired because the ship was so uncomfortable.

Jim Lovell lost 14 pounds. Fred Haise got a kidney infection and started running a fever.

After leaving lunar orbit and approaching Earth, *13* then needed to power up the LM again to make a second course correction. The window to land safely on Earth was very small, and it's hard enough to hit it at the best of times, but flying the ship from the LM, without any computer assistance or electronic guidance, was going to take superhuman piloting skill. Failure would mean certain death for the crew.

Lovell and Haise grabbed the LM controls as they received radio transmissions from NASA. Lovell controlled the pitch and the acceleration, but Haise controlled the yaw (the craft's side-to-side movement), which is completely wild to think about. Imagine trying to play a shooting or flying game on Xbox, except you only control the left stick and your buddy controls the right stick on the same controller. It is not easy!

Because *13* couldn't afford to restart the computer to calculate reentry, the crew were going to have to navigate the same way old sailing ships did: by looking at the stars. As long as they kept the top-left corner of the Earth in the front window, and the sun in the window directly above them, they would be on the right track. It wasn't a precise form of navigation, but it was the best they had.

Jim Lovell lined up the Earth and ignited the thrusters on the LM. A huge jet of flame exploded out the back of the thrusters, catapulting the *Apollo 13* spacecraft toward home.

Ten seconds later, Houston reported that *13* had hit the target within two degrees. The crew couldn't have done it better if they'd had the guidance computer in front of them.

After six long days in space, *Apollo 13* was now beginning its approach toward Earth's atmosphere. But success still wasn't guaranteed.

LMs don't have heat shields, and because the heat from reentry would burn them to pieces, the crew were going to have to move back to the CSM, boot it up, and hope for the best. Crews on the ground, assisted by guys like astronaut Ken Mattingly, had run hundreds of simulations trying to figure out how to get the CSM up and running on minimal power. By the time *Apollo 13* reached the atmosphere, they had a pretty good idea of how to do that. But there were still a lot of questions.

First, remember the condensation making the equipment panels wet? Water and electronics do not go together. Even one malfunction could short out the entire CSM and leave it dead in space. Second, nobody knew how badly the explosion had damaged the CSM. Even one small crack in the heat shield would be deadly during reentry. Third, there was the issue of the parachutes. Were they damaged? Would they deploy and open correctly? Were they frozen into ice cubes? Nobody knew.

Across the world, humanity came together to wish the best for the astronauts. The pope led prayers at the Vatican. People gathered around televisions and radios in their homes, churches, and other meeting areas from Los Angeles to London, hoping that this amazing saga would have a happy ending.

Seven days after lifting off from Cape Canaveral, Jim Lovell, Jack Swigert, and Fred Haise ejected the LM from the damaged CSM, powered up the CM, and began their descent toward Earth. They hurtled toward the surface at hundreds of miles per hour, attempting a daring landing with only a minimal amount of electrical power. All around them, ice and water melted, dripping down onto the astronauts so rapidly it must have felt like rain.

There's a three-minute radio blackout whenever a spacecraft attempts reentry. News cameras and crewmen aboard the rescue ship USS *Iwo Jima* scanned the skies, straining to catch any sign of the CM. Families held their breath as they stared at their televisions. What would happen to these brave astronauts?

Then, through the clouds, three bright red parachutes appeared, gently bringing *Apollo 13* out of the sky.

A huge cheer erupted on the deck of the *Iwo Jima* and across the world.

They'd made it.

Apollo 13 splashed down safely in the Pacific Ocean just four miles from its target. Rescue helicopters from the *Iwo Jima* brought Jim

Lovell, Jack Swigert, and Fred Haise back home, where they were celebrated for their bravery, perseverance, and heroism in the face of almost certain death.

The *Apollo 13* mission is considered by NASA to be a "successful failure," meaning that the crew had failed to land on the moon. But NASA had learned so much during the operation, including techniques that would go on to aid in

Mission Control celebrates the safe return of *Apollo 13*.

the development of new mission protocols and better technological advancements for future missions. In the end, despite this mission being a pretty Epic Fail, *Apollo 13* and its crew have since gone down as one of the greatest survival stories in the history of our species.

CHAPTER 13
The Final Frontier

1975

"We thought they were pretty aggressive people and . . . they probably thought we were monsters. So we very quickly broke through that, because when you deal with people that are in the same line of work as you are, and you're around them for a short time, why, you discover that, well, they're human beings."

—Vance Brand

By 1972, the space race was winding down. The Americans had landed on the moon multiple times, and the Soviet space program had abandoned its moon program and shifted instead toward a new strategy of building space stations for research and exploration.

The Cold War was starting to "thaw out"

politically as well. In May 1972, US president Richard Nixon traveled to Moscow to meet Soviet premier Leonid Brezhnev. It was the first time that a US president had ever visited the capital of the USSR. The purpose of the mission was simple: to begin a new policy between the two world superpowers known as *détente* (a French word meaning "the easing of hostilities"). Nixon was moving US soldiers out of Vietnam, opening trade with the Soviets, and the two leaders were now going to try to start a period of cooperation rather than hostility.

One of the most visible examples of *détente* would be a joint US-Soviet space program known as the Apollo-Soyuz Test Project. Both countries had space stations in orbit (the Soviet Salyut and the American Skylab) and were progressing in their exploration. The Apollo-Soyuz Test Project would involve a US ship and a Soviet ship docking in outer space in a symbolic expression of peace between the two countries. If that doesn't seem like a big deal to you, keep in mind that a lot of US astronauts had flown jet fighters in combat against Soviet MiGs in the Korean and Vietnam Wars.

Display of the Apollo-Soyuz capsules docking at the Smithsonian Air and Space Museum in Washington DC

The Apollo spacecraft would be commanded by astronaut Tom Stafford, and the Soviet Soyuz craft would be commanded by cosmonaut Alexei Leonov, the first human ever to successfully perform a space walk (EVA). Three Apollo astronauts and two Soyuz cosmonauts would move to a training facility in Houston, where they'd spend the next two years preparing for their historic mission.

Getting a group of people to work together and crew a spaceship was hard enough, but now you had five guys who didn't speak the same language and were from two countries that had spent the last thirty years hating each other's guts. For

The Apollo-Soyuz mission crews

three decades, the United States and the USSR were one bad day away from incinerating Earth in a nuclear war, so you can imagine there might have been a little bit of pressure on these guys, considering that their mission was to serve as a beacon of peace between these two countries.

The first hurdle was for both crews to learn the other's language. Tom Stafford was from Oklahoma, and he had a pretty hard-core accent, so the Soviets (who had studied English in school) had a tough time understanding him at first. Stafford spoke a little Russian, but not much. It also doesn't help that the two languages don't even use the same alphabets. Eventually, after weeks of working together, the two crews cobbled together a common language that they jokingly referred to as "Oklahomski."

After two long years of training, simulations, and practice, the mission was finally ready to begin in July 1975. The Soviets launched their Soyuz craft from Kazakhstan, and seven and a half hours later the Americans launched an

Apollo spaceship from Cape Canaveral in Florida. After two days in orbit, the two ships located each other and began the delicate docking procedure. Both countries were watching live on television; failure could have potentially been a bad omen for US-Soviet relations.

The Soyuz and Apollo spacecrafts linked up in Earth orbit on July 17, 1975. The Soviet crew went to the hatch and knocked for the Americans to let them in. Tom Stafford responded by yelling (in perfect Russian), "Who's there?" The Soviets laughed, the Americans opened the hatch, and the two greatest space-faring countries on Earth were sharing a single spaceship for the first time in history. Two countries that were recently enemies were now shaking hands and hugging on worldwide television. It was the first step in what is now a concerted effort by all the countries on Earth to work as one and explore our universe together.

The cosmonauts and astronauts ate together and hung out in the ship for two days. They talked on the phone to Brezhnev and President Gerald Ford, exchanged presents, and told stories. Apollo commander Tom Stafford played a song he'd brought with him. He'd asked American country music star Conway Twitty to record his hit song "Hello Darlin'" with the lyrics translated into Russian, and both crews sat together and listened to it before they undocked.

This was a momentous step toward peace between the United States and the USSR, but it was just the beginning of the world working together on space travel, exploration, and scientific discovery. More joint missions would follow, first to the Soviet space station Mir, and then later to the International Space Station, which was launched in 1998 from parts brought up by US space shuttles and Soyuz and Proton rockets from the Russian Federation. Nowadays, NASA, the Russian Roscosmos, and space agencies from Canada, Japan, India, and China all work together on countless missions to space for research and discovery.

A lot has happened since we put a man on the moon. The Berlin Wall fell, the Cold War ended, the Internet was invented, and gluten-free English muffins became a thing. Nearly fifty years after Neil Armstrong's "One small step,"

Astronaut Mike Hopkins takes a "space selfie" during an EVA from the International Space Station on Christmas Eve, 2013.

mankind has taken multiple giant leaps in science and technology: from the space shuttle program to reusable rockets, Mars rovers, and probing deep space in search of potentially habitable planets. Generations of scientists and innovators have been inspired by these brave pioneers of the Space Age. But the moon was not the end; it was just the beginning!

And we're still only just getting started.

TIMELINE

1895   Tsiolkovsky becomes the first engineer to come up with a rocket equation for escaping Earth's gravity

1903   The Wright Brothers successfully create the first airplane

1926   Robert Goddard successfully launches the world's first liquid-fueled rocket

1942   Wernher von Braun's first successful test launch of the V-2 rocket in Germany

1945   The first atomic bomb—Trinity test site in Los Alamos, New Mexico

1945   WWII ends with the bombing of Hiroshima and Nagasaki

1946   Von Braun begins working for the United States

1947   Hermes rocket flies wildly off course from the White Sands test site and lands in Mexico

1947   Chuck Yeager becomes the first pilot to reach Mach 1 and break the sound barrier in the X-1

1947   The Soviets launch their first V-2

1947   The Cold War begins

1949   The USSR tests its first nuclear weapon

1952   The United States detonates the first hydrogen bomb

1957   Sputnik is launched by the Soviets

1957   The Soviets put first dog into space

1957	TV-3 Vanguard rocket fails
1958	US launches its first satellite into orbit: Explorer 1
1958	NASA is signed into existence
1959	The Mercury astronauts are selected
1961	Soviet cosmonaut Yuri Gagarin becomes the first human in space, aboard *Vostok 1*
1961	Alan Shepard becomes the first American in space, aboard *Freedom 7*
1962	John Glenn makes three orbits around the Earth in *Friendship 7*
1965	The "corned beef sandwich incident" aboard *Gemini 3*
1966	Neil Armstrong's successful rendezvous with the *Agena* during *Gemini 8*
1967	*Apollo 1* tragedy
1967	*Soyuz 1* tragedy
1967	Venera 4—Soviet probe reaches Venus
1968	*Apollo 8* orbits the moon
1969	*Apollo 11*—Neil Armstrong and Buzz Aldrin successfully land on the moon and return home safely to Earth
1970	*Apollo 13*—a successful failure
1972	*Apollo 17*—the last men on the moon
1972	NASA's space shuttle program begins
1973	NASA's first space station, Skylab, becomes operational
1973	NASA's Mariner 10 probe flies past Venus and Mercury
1975	Apollo-Soyuz—the first US-Soviet joint mission

ACKNOWLEDGMENTS

The authors would like to thank our editors, Simon Boughton and Connie Hsu, for believing in this project and giving us the opportunity to write it, and to our agent, Farley Chase of Chase Literary, for helping us work out all the details to make this happen. Thanks also to our editor, Mekisha Telfer, and our copy editors, Sally Doherty and Tracy Koontz, for their excellent work helping us get this book into shape. And, most of all, we would like to thank you, the reader, for taking the time to read this book! Without your support, none of this could be possible. We really hope you liked it.

Erik would like to first thank Ben for the amazing opportunity to work on this project—it really is a dream come true. I, of course, want to acknowledge all my friends and family for their support over the years, as well as any- and everyone who has ever encouraged me to keep on writing.

A very special shout-out to: David Kowalski (for helping to brainstorm the concept of writing about historical failures), Chris Carroll (for introducing me to blogging), Justin Ache (for helping me redesign my website and hosting it), James Lester (for inspiring me to keep the history blog going), Neil Sindicich (for giving me the opportunity to build up my online writing portfolio), Max Michaels (for my first writing gig in print), Damian Fox (for pushing me to pursue publication and helping me put together my first pitch), John Wesley Moody (my college history professor), Jason Whitmarsh (my humanities professor), my Patreon patrons who have financially supported my blogging habit over the years, and to Dani Slader—who put up with me every step of the way. Finally, I want to thank Meg—for her endless support and love during the craziest year of my life.

(If I missed anyone, it's only because I'm already way over my word count.)

Ben would like to thank the amazing and wonderful Thaís Melo for being the reason I wake up excited and happy for each new day. You make my life better, and I love you always. I'd also like to thank my family and friends whom I relied on and counted on so much for support during the writing process this time around: Mom, Dad, Clay, John, Matt, Brian, Alyssa, Quynh-An, and all of my D&D crew.

BIBLIOGRAPHY

Aaseng, Nathan. *World History Series: The Space Race.* San Diego, CA: Lucent Books, 2002.

Aerospace: aerospace.org.

Impey, Chris. *Beyond: Our Future in Space.* New York: W. W. Norton & Company, Inc., 2015.

Kennedy Space Center: kennedyspacecenter.com.

Kranz, Gene. *Failure Is Not an Option: Mission Control from Mercury to Apollo 13 and Beyond.* New York: Simon & Schuster, Inc., 2000.

NASA: nasa.gov.

Nelson, Craig. *Rocket Men: The Epic Story of the First Men on the Moon.* New York: Viking Penguin, 2009.

Sparrow, Giles, Judith John & Chris McNab. *The Illustrated Encyclopedia of Space & Space Exploration.* London, UK: Amber Books Ltd, 2014.

Teitel, Amy Shira. *Breaking the Chains of Gravity: The Story of Spaceflight before NASA.* New York: Bloomsbury Publishing, 2016.

INDEX

Numbers in **bold** indicate pages with illustrations

PHOTO CREDITS

Page 8: Courtesy of United States Civil Air Patrol; **14:** Courtesy of NASA; **22:** Courtesy of National Nuclear Security Administration / Nevada Site Office; **27:** Courtesy of United States Air Force; **28–29:** Courtesy of NASA / JPL-Caltech; **34:** Courtesy of NASA; **38:** Courtesy of U.S. Navy; **47:** Courtesy of The British Newspaper Archive; **50:** Courtesy of NASA; **53:** Courtesy of NASA; **62:** Courtesy of NASA; **64:** Courtesy of NASA; **77:** Courtesy of NASA; **78:** Courtesy of NASA; **82:** Courtesy of NASA; **95:** Courtesy of NASA; **102:** Courtesy of NASA; **111:** Courtesy of NASA; **112–113:** Courtesy of NASA; **121:** Courtesy of NASA; **131:** Courtesy of NASA; **135:** Courtesy of Toytoy at English Wikipedia; **136:** Courtesy of NASA; **141:** Courtesy of NASA.